AF143797

BOOK ANALYSIS

By Benjamin Taylor

Tropic of Cancer
BY HENRY MILLER

HENRY MILLER 9

TROPIC OF CANCER 13

SUMMARY 17

Life in Paris
A new job
Fillmore
Life away from Paris

CHARACTERS 23

Henry Miller
Van Norden
Carl
Mona

ANALYSIS 29

Paris
Time and timelessness
Historical context
Sex, ecstasy and philosophy

FURTHER REFLECTION 37

FURTHER READING 41

HENRY MILLER

AMERICAN NOVELIST

- **Born in New York in 1891.**
- **Died in California in 1980.**
- **Notable works:**
  - *Black Spring* (1936), novel
  - *Tropic of Capricorn* (1939), novel
  - *The Colossus of Maroussi* (1941), travelogue

Henry Miller is perhaps one of the most innovative American novelists of the 20th century, who inspired generations of writers with his work. He is most famous for his novels, which are often highly autobiographical, experimental and open about sex. Miller was born in New York at the end of the 19th century, and left America to focus on his career as a writer, moving to Paris, where he wrote *Tropic of Cancer*, and Greece, before settling in California, where he would remain until his death in 1980. Despite being widely celebrated, Miller was a controversial figure during his lifetime, with many of his works, including *Tropic of Cancer*, being banned in the US for their sexual explicitness and general sordidness. It is this sexual liberation, along with his experiments with form and style, which makes Miller such an important and influential American literary figure.

TROPIC OF CANCER

DOWN AND OUT IN PARIS

- **Genre:** novel
- **Reference edition:** Miller, H. (1993) *Tropic of Cancer*. London: Flamingo.
- **1st edition:** 1934
- **Themes:** sex, Paris, war, modernism, art, poverty, friendship, philosophy, writing

Tropic of Cancer was published in 1934 and is based on Henry Miller's time living in Paris as a down-and-out. It centres around a fictional version of Miller himself and his bohemian lifestyle, along with a set of literary and artist friends said to be based on real-life people. The events in the novel are episodic and autobiographical, and many of them revolve around sex and the narrator's various encounters with women. The novel was notorious when it was first published, being banned in the US for its sexual explicitness and becoming the subject of several high-profile obscenity trials relating to what was considered its pornographic content. As a result of its controversial subject matter, the novel was not published in the US until 1961, but it found success abroad in the meantime. Though initially difficult to get hold of, *Tropic of Cancer* enjoyed a largely positive critical reception, attracting notable admirers including George Orwell, who praised Miller and the novel in his famous 1940 essay *Inside the Whale*.

SUMMARY

LIFE IN PARIS

We are introduced to the narrator – who is Miller himself – living in the Villa Borghese in Paris with a friend of his named Boris. We join him two years into his stay in Paris and are introduced to his various friends and well-wishers, including Borowski, Mona (his estranged wife who lives in America) and Tania, with whom he is deeply enamoured but who has run off with a playwright named Sylvester. His life in Paris is an impoverished and excessive one, which he manages to keep afloat through the charity of his friends and various odd writing jobs. He whiles away much of his time writing and going out drinking and to brothels with his friends Carl and Van Norden, womanisers and aspiring writers in turn.

He walks the streets finding various ways to satisfy his appetite and libido – remembering along the way various incidents that have befallen him and people he has met, such as a particularly memorable prostitute called Ginette. The narrator often remembers Mona, who is living in America, and wonders at the decaying nature of the post-war world around him, seeing the fate of modern Europe to be an inexorable march towards the end.

A NEW JOB

After a string of jobs and periods of unemployment, Miller finds work as a proof-reader; a strenuous job which he nonetheless finds himself to be good at. Meanwhile, Tania moves back to Paris from Russia, and she and Miller continue their affair. She asks him to move to Russia with her, but he declines. When he loses his job, Miller pays off his bills and manages to survive by making and sponging from new friends, including artists named Kruger and Mark Swift, as well as a man named Fillmore, who takes Miller out to the country where they go to a dinner party, get drunk and go to a brothel with an ex-sailor named Collins.

On their return to Paris, Miller is gifted a few hundred francs by Collins, and as such parts ways with a spring in his step. He begins looking for cheap accommodation in the hope of rationing his money, but is prevented from doing so when he meets two women – one Irish and the other a Norwegian midwife, grieving for her recently dead child. He goes back to her apartment with her and propositions her, exchanging a 100-franc note for the night. She is distracted as her mother is dying downstairs and he exits, taking the money with him.

FILLMORE

Later in the summer, he has landed on his feet staying with a friend of his named Fillmore, who now has space in his apartment after the final departure of a lingering relationship. Miller is happy, with good food, drink and a space to finish his novel provided for him – though Fillmore often wishes to read his work uninvited. One day, Fillmore returns from work with a woman named Macha, who claims to be a Russian princess who has got herself lost in Paris by faking her suicide. Fillmore laboriously attempts to seduce her while she stays with them, though she is wildly impulsive and, as it turns out is suffering from gonorrhoea.

Macha eventually moves out, leaving Henry and Fillmore alone in the apartment. They while away the evenings discussing America, Paris and the literature of the two places as he makes increasing progress on his book. He considers great writers before him, his own life and his relationship with Mona. When on the cusp of having sex with a prostitute one night in Fillmore's apartment, he imagines her body to be the decaying earth. In a long and meandering explanation of his ideas about the world, he claims to want to embrace the inhuman in him, the madness and delirium of the wild human condition, and to pursue the things which cause ecstasy in life.

LIFE AWAY FROM PARIS

Miller and Fillmore pass the Christmas period drinking champagne and lounging about his apartment. They go to Mass one day, and Miller tells us of his contempt for world religions and some of the reasons in his past for this mistrust as they are kicked out of the church by the priest. Miller has accepted a position as an exchange professor of English in the more provincial city of Dijon. He is wholly dismayed by the place, however, despising the eerie cultishness of the school and the surrounding city, as well as the boredom of having no money in a place where no fun can be had.

In desperation, he finds a way out through a letter from Carl, who tells him he has a room spare at his hotel. On arriving back in Paris, Miller learns that Fillmore is in trouble, having apparently simultaneously impregnated and given gonorrhoea to a French woman named Ginette. He has a mental breakdown and is taken to a mental hospital – while the parents of the girl plan their engagement. Ginette is jealous and obsessive, and there are doubts as to whether she is pregnant at all. Eventually, Fillmore's situation is so dire that Miller convinces him to return to America, something which he is sad about but eventually consents to.

CHARACTERS

HENRY MILLER

The main protagonist of the novel is a fictionalised version of Miller himself, reflective of the immersive first-person experience which it tries to convey. Miller is self-described as "a hopeless lecher" (p. 175), and spends the novel moving from friend to friend, doing various odd jobs in the meantime in a bid to be fed and to fuel his excessive lifestyle of boozing and prostitution. Miller is American and reflects often on the place and its central ideologies, as well as his reasons for living abroad: "I don't ask to go back to America, to be put in double harness again, to work the treadmill. No, I prefer to be a poor man of Europe. God knows, I am poor enough; it only remains to be a man" (p. 76). He is furthermore haunted by the memory of his wife, Mona, who lives back in the USA and who is said to be based on Miller's second wife June.

Miller therefore appears to be in Paris in order to follow a lifestyle in line with the ideology which runs through the novel – which embraces the chaotic and unseemly in the world in the pursuit of that which brings 'ecstasy': "I join my slime, my excrement, my madness, my ecstasy to the great circuit which flows through the subterranean vaults of the flesh" (p. 255). Miller spends much of the novel experiencing these ecstasies in a desperate attempt to counter what he sees as a modern world hurtling towards self-destruction and decay.

VAN NORDEN

Van Norden is one of Miller's close writer friends living in Paris, who is primarily defined in the novel by his near-sociopathic womanising. Indeed, so dominated is his personality by this trait that he becomes almost caricature-like: "I like Van Norden, but I do not share his opinion of himself. I do not agree, for instance, that he is a philosopher, or a thinker. He is cunt-struck, that's all. And he will never be a writer" (p. 12). Van Norden brings women to his hotel room almost every single night, objectifying and degrading many of them and seemingly having no emotional connection to them. Indeed, at one point in the novel, Miller himself is present at one of these sessions and compares the joyless and mindless sexual act that he witnesses to "a machine which has slipped its cogs" (p. 148). Van Norden is vain, self-obsessed, and reveals an insight into the psychology of his treatment of women late in the book: "that's all I want of them – to forget myself" (p. 134).

CARL

Carl is another of Miller's writer friends living in Paris who often accompanies him on excursions to the various bistros and whorehouses he frequents. Unlike Van Norden, Carl is respected as a writer by Miller, who claims of him, along with his other friend Boris: "The only writers about me for whom I have any respect, at present, are Carl and Boris. They are possessed. They glow inwardly with a white flame. They are mad and tone deaf. They are sufferers" (p. 12). Carl, who is originally from Arizona, is often aloof, described by Miller as "a snob, an aristocratic little prick who lives in a dementia praecox kingdom all his own. "I hate Paris" he whines. "All these stupid people playing cards all day"" (pp. 56-7). Despite this diatribe, they are long-term companions, and Carl often spots Miller for food and drink. In the novel, Carl notably has an affair with both an older woman and an underage girl.

MONA

Mona is Miller's estranged wife in the novel, who lives in America and haunts his memories. She often seems on the brink of coming to visit him in Paris, though she never does and she remains an idealised, spectre-like character always on the edge of his mind. Mona is said to be based on Miller's real-life second wife, June Miller, who appears biographically in many of his works. As a character presented only through memory, Mona is of course heavily defined by Miller's own perspective, and as such she is romanticised and comes to represent a murky past that is never properly revealed. He is clearly still deeply enamoured with her and indeed pictures her far more romantically than any of the other women that he encounters in the novel: "Close together, America three thousand miles away. I never want to see it again. To have her here in bed with me, breathing on me, her hair in my mouth"

(p. 27). Her presence in his mind is a consistent theme throughout the novel, appearing in quiet moments of his otherwise chaotic lifestyle, perhaps proving that despite his ideological pursuit of pleasure, sentiment is something Miller is unable to be fully rid of: "I had been reconciled to this life without her, and yet if I thought about her only for a minute it was enough to pierce the bone and marrow of my contentment and shove me back again into the agonizing gutter of my wretched past" (p. 182).

ANALYSIS

PARIS

Paris is historically known as a place of teeming literary culture, and in the 1920s and 30s it was renowned for being the worldwide hub of expatriate writers and artists living bohemian lives. Following in the footsteps of fellow Americans such as Ernest Hemingway, F. Scott Fitzgerald and Ezra Pound, as well as other writers such as James Joyce and George Orwell, Miller moved to Paris in 1930, where he began to write *Tropic of Cancer*. Paris, and the unique social and artistic circumstances that surround his time there, come to play a major part in shaping the novel, with Miller often portraying the duality of the city as both a place steeped in history, beauty and life and a place of poverty and degeneracy. He talks of a Paris in which "the humblest mortal alive must feel that he dwells in paradise" (p. 74) and yet one which also "grows inside you like a cancer and grows and grows until you are eaten away by it" (p. 184). Indeed, the city acts as a sort of petri dish, in which the chaotic and bohemian nature of Miller's lifestyle there supplements his ideological aims and allows him to write the novel by essentially living his art, just as Paris itself comes to represent the chaos and exhilaration of life. Paris as a place then also comes to be seen as something which is part of people, an obsession: "when you've suffered and endured things here, it's then that Paris takes hold of you, grabs you by the balls" (p. 176).

TIME AND TIMELESSNESS

In keeping with the ethereal, chaotic nature of Miller's lifestyle in *Tropic of Cancer*, a timeless, unregulated air runs through the novel, representing the cyclical and unregimented disorder of Parisian life. Miller notes early on that "it is the twenty-somethingth of October. I no longer keep track of the date" (p. 10), and indeed, other than vague references to seasonal changes, many of the events in the book are random and undated. He goes on to talk of his own mental condition: "everything that belongs to the past seems to have fallen into the sea; I have memories, but the images have lost their vividness, they seem dead and desultory, like time-bitten mummies stuck in a quagmire" (p. 157). The novel is therefore resolutely set in the present, and indeed this reflects Miller's intentions of recording the free-flowing realities of his day-to-day life and ideas. The events in the book, none of which are ever referred back to, are episodic and rarely connected, making it cyclical and immediate. He claims near the end of the novel that "I love scripts that flow, be they hieratic, esoteric, perverse, polymorph, or unilateral. I love everything that brings us back to the beginning where there is never end" (p. 259). Nothing has changed by the end of the novel, certainly not in terms of Miller's circumstances: we leave him still pondering his life in Paris in much the state that we find him in at the start.

HISTORICAL CONTEXT

Europe in the 1930s was a place in the grip of a changing world, producing increasingly unfamiliar technological and artistic advances and still reeling from the ideological, social and economic effects of the First World War (1914-18) which obliterated the central infrastructure of many of its leading nations. This, as well as the worldwide economic catastrophe of the Great Depression, caused a massive increase in poverty, and its effects could be felt around the continent – Miller for example noting that "Paris is filled with poor people – the proudest and filthiest lot of beggars that ever walked the earth, it seems to me" (p. 74). Due to new technologies and methods of mass production, day-to-day life was also changing in a drastic way, and a burgeoning consumerism was making its way into Western society. It is because of such historical factors that Miller sees the world in such an awful state in the novel, as he claims that "For a hundred years or more, the world, *our* world has been dying" (p. 33). There are constant references to a world that is decaying, its future dominated by machinery: "the earth is moving out of orbit, the axis has shifted; from the north the snow blows down in huge knife-blue drifts. A new ice age is setting in" (p. 169). This view is reflective of the fears of the time, a backlash against the rapid technological and ideological shifts that were changing society.

Though the novel was published in 1934, the worrying predictions about society's future, images of decay and degeneration and the search for ideological progress can be seen in the context of the Second World War (1939-45) – with the Nazi Party and Fascist movements elsewhere in Europe gaining ground rapidly and the premonition of global conflict becoming more and more realistic.

SEX, ECSTASY AND PHILOSOPHY

It is clear from the start of *Tropic of Cancer* that Miller intends to make a statement. He claims that the novel is "a prolonged insult, a gob of spit in the face of art, a kick in the pants to God, Man, Destiny, Time, Love, Beauty" (p. 10). In the combination of his life and experiences, it therefore also comes to be an exposition of his philosophies and the way that he lives his life in the face of what he sees as a rapidly deteriorating world: "Everything around us is crumbling, crumbling and the warm body under the warm velvet is aching for me" (p. 26). Indeed, Miller is clearly an advocate of the enjoyment of pleasurable pursuits, partying and using prostitutes heavily throughout the novel. It becomes clear, however, that his actions are almost a deliberate reaction to the world around him, as he claims

"One must burrow into life again in order to put on flesh. The word must become flesh; the soul thirsts. On whatever crumb my eye fastens, I will pounce and devour. If to live is the paramount thing then I will live, even if I must become a cannibal." (p. 104). It is through pleasure and art that he derives meaning from the world – notably referencing a score of artists, poets and writers throughout the novel – and his almost obsessive pursuit of sex seems to derive from this, as he cries in a reverie late in the novel "Do anything, but let it bring joy" (p. 253).

FURTHER REFLECTION

SOME QUESTIONS TO THINK ABOUT...

- Think about the controversy surrounding the novel when it was first published – should the novel be considered pornographic? How do we separate pornography and art?
- Think about the way that many of the novel's female characters are portrayed. Would this be deemed appropriate in contemporary liberal society?
- Due to the episodic nature of the book, can it be considered a picaresque novel?
- Mona, who is apparently based on Miller's real-life second wife June Miller, is only presented through his memory. Does this distort the nature of her character at all?
- How much can we trust Miller as an autobiographical narrator? Is it possible that he has distorted the events of the novel?
- What do you think it is about Paris at this time in history that attracted so many writers and artists?

- The novel is set in the heart of Europe in between the two world wars. How is this unique historical circumstance reflected in the novel?
- What is the difference between sex and love in the novel? Compare Miller's portrayal of Mona to the other female characters he encounters.
- How does Miller's innovative use of syntax affect our reading of the novel?

We want to hear from you!
Leave a comment on your online library
and share your favourite books on social media!

FURTHER READING

REFERENCE EDITION

- Miller, H. (1993) *Tropic of Cancer*. London: Flamingo.

ADAPTATIONS

- *Tropic of Cancer*. (1970) [Film]. Joseph Strick. Dir. US: Paramount Pictures.

Although the editor makes every effort to verify the accuracy of the information published, BrightSummaries.com accepts no responsibility for the content of this book.

www.brightsummaries.com

Ebook EAN: 9782808019118

Paperback EAN: 9782808019125

Legal Deposit: D/2019/12603/122

Cover: © Primento

Digital conception by Primento, the digital partner of publishers.